AMERICAN INDIAN RADIO VOICES

by Colleen Keane

ZB **Zaner-Bloser**

Columbus, Ohio

TABLE OF CONTENTS

Introduction

In your neighborhood, your next-door neighbor may be just steps away. In Indian country, the closest neighbor is often miles away.

Your home may have several phones; one may be in your kitchen, one may be in your living room, and one may be in your dining room. In Indian country, many homes don't even have one phone. Some homes do not have electricity.

You may be able to use the Internet in many different places. Maybe you surf the Internet in your home. Maybe you surf in a classroom. Or maybe you surf in the library.

Most American Indian homes are far away from towns, cities, and libraries. Only about 70 percent of American Indian homes have phones. Only ten percent have Internet access. You may wonder how people can get by without a phone or the Internet. How can they do well in school? How can they get information? How can they let others know what they have to say? How do they make their voices heard?

This book will tell you how American Indians were silenced for many years. It will explain what they are doing to get information and make their voices heard—on the radio!

CHAPTER 1

From Foot Runners to Radio Stars

Imagine running all day long. That's what the American Indian foot runner did. He traveled miles to bring news and information to people. Just like the modern mail carrier, the foot runner delivered news and information in rain, hail, sleet, and snow. The foot runner ran from one village to another. The foot runner helped to make American Indian voices heard.

In the 1880s, when the United States government forced American Indians onto reservations, the tradition of the foot runner ended. During this time, Indian reservations were similar to concentration camps. A concentration camp is a place where people are forced to stay, or be punished or killed. When American Indians were forced to live on reservations, their voices were silenced.

The United States government also believed that American Indians should speak English and not their own native languages. Up until the 1970s, American Indian children were forced to leave their families. The idea was that they would learn English and forget their first languages.

They were also forced to attend boarding schools many miles away from their homes. These schools were so far away from their homes that the children didn't go home for many months.

Imagine how you would feel if someone you had never seen before took you away from your parents when you were a very young child. Imagine if your parents couldn't do anything about it.

Then, imagine that you can't understand the strange people at the school when they talk to you. They speak a language you have never heard before.

Today, Navajo children like Skylin from the Navajo Ramah community, go to school in their own communities.

When you speak your own language at school, you are punished. You have never been treated this way before. School's very hurtful, confusing, and lonely. Because of this treatment, many American Indian children lost the ability to speak their own language. When they went home, they couldn't understand their parents or grandparents. Much of their history and culture was lost to them. It was another way that American Indians have been kept from having a voice in this country.

By the 1970s, American Indian voices had been mostly silenced. Little true information about American Indians made its way into American society. By this time, many non-Indians thought American Indian tribes didn't even exist anymore. Information about American Indians was seldom included in schoolbooks or shown on television.

When American Indians were mentioned, it wasn't a true picture. Let's look at early television, from before you were born. One of the first American Indian actors was Jay Silverheels. He starred in *The Lone Ranger.* It was a television program about a masked cowboy who helped people in trouble. Jay Silverheels played Tonto. He was the Lone Ranger's loyal **sidekick**.

Because Jay Silverheels was one of the only American Indians on television or radio at the time, people thought that most American Indians were like Tonto. This is called **stereotyping.** Like any actor, Jay Silverheels was just playing a role.

In real life, Jay Silverheels was an athlete and a businessman. As an active member of his community, he helped many American Indian students. He founded the Indian Actors' Workshop in 1963. Jay Silverheels wanted people to see more American Indians on television. He wanted people to hear their voices on the radio. He wanted more American Indian voices to be heard. Jay Silverheels started efforts that other people continue today.

Jay Silverheels, an American Indian actor and activist

CHAPTER 2

American Indian Nations and the New Foot Runners

After 1934, American Indian tribes took control of their lands. This was when a law called the Indian Reorganization Act passed.

Today, if you drive with your family to an American Indian community, you will enter another country. It is a **sovereign nation,** just like France or England.

Once you are on Indian land, you have to abide by the laws of the Indian nation. Most of these laws are the same as laws that you are used to. There are speeding laws, there are laws against littering, and there are laws about going to school. Today, American Indian children go to school in their own communities.

As American Indian tribes rebuilt their communities, they began to look for a new kind of foot runner. By 1970, they had started using a communication system that could run from one village to another and over one mountain to the next.

It was the radio station!

Like foot runners, radio stations allowed American Indians to communicate over great distances.

Bernie Bustos, who works for the Ramah Navajo School Board, points up at the KTDB radio tower in Pinehill, New Mexico.

Since the 1970s, several American Indian tribes have built radio stations. They **broadcast** from the Arctic villages of Alaska and from the valleys and mesas of Arizona and California. American Indian communities have radio stations on the damp coast of Washington, in the high deserts of New Mexico, and in the wide plains of Montana. American Indian stations are all over!

Close-up of a Navajo student reading on air at KTDB

It was the United States government that forced American Indians onto reservations and created policies to punish children for speaking their own languages. Ironically, this was the same government that gave American Indians a radio voice. The government gave tribes money to build radio stations and put up towers across the country.

Radio stations have become very good foot runners. They have given American Indian people information, music, and entertainment. They have also become a way for people in communities to be heard.

Tribes use Indian radio stations to communicate about everyday things such as weather forecasts and school closings. They provide information about voting, health, education, and culture. Indian radio has also helped to save lives, especially in very remote places such as Bethel, Alaska, that can be hit by sudden, dangerous weather. Today, Indian radio also plays a valuable role in helping to preserve American Indian languages.

Putting up new radio towers and starting radio stations is not easy. Still, many communities succeed in doing this. In the next chapter, you'll learn about radio stations in three different communities.

CHAPTER 3

American Indian Radio Stations

Let's learn about three community radio stations and the places they broadcast.

KYUK, Bethel, Alaska

The very first American Indian public radio station began broadcasting in 1971. It was KYUK in Bethel, Alaska. It is owned by the Inuit (in•yoo•it) people. Bethel is located 90 miles from the Bering Sea on the west coast of Alaska. If you live in Bethel and want to go to a movie, you need to travel 400 miles to Anchorage. The only ways into the area during the summer are by boat or plane. In winter, the only way in is by plane and even the planes can land only if the weather is good enough. The radio station is one of the only ways the Inuit people's voices are heard.

KBRW 680 AM

KOTZ 720 AM KZPA 900 AM

KNSA 930 AM

KIYU 910 AM

KCUK 88.1 FM   ALASKA   YUKON TERRITORY

KYUK 640 AM KNBA 90.3 FM

KUHB 91.9 FM

KSDP 830 AM   Gulf of Alaska

American Indian radio stations in Alaska

KTDB, Ramah, New Mexico

In 1972, a band of the Navajo (nahv•uh•**hoh**) Nation called Ramah (**ray**•muh), who live in Pinehill, New Mexico, began broadcasting on KTDB. The station is owned and operated by the Ramah Navajo School Board.

The Navajo Nation is one of the largest American Indian tribes in the country. It has more than 300,000 tribal members. The Navajo Nation covers parts of Arizona, Utah, and New Mexico.

To reach KTDB, you and your family would drive west from Albuquerque until you reach Grants, New Mexico. From Grants, the road curves through and around mountains, valleys, and green hills. Signs direct you to a wolf reserve and a bat cave. When you have gone about 60 miles, you will see a turnoff at a bend in the road and a sign that says Ramah.

A road sign to Ramah Navajo community

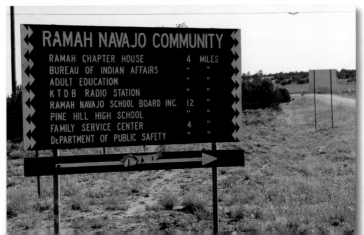

The village has a school, a gas station, and a grocery store. There is no department store, electronics store, or mall. There *are* running streams, mountain trails, and glorious sunsets. The center of the community is the Ramah Navajo School and the radio station, KTDB. The radio station is like the community newspaper. It is called the Voice of the People. It keeps people informed about local, regional, and national news in both the English and Navajo languages. It also provides entertainment. There is a mix of music, from Native American to hip-hop, rock-and-roll, and country and western.

KUYI, Polacca, Arizona

One of the newest American Indian radio stations on the air is KUYI in Polacca, Arizona. It is on the Hopi Indian Reservation. Like other Indian radio stations, it carries a mix of programming, including music, information about tribal and village governments, and live coverage of high school basketball games.

Other American Indian Radio Stations

By 2006, 31 American Indian tribes operated public radio stations across the country.

Native voices can be heard over public radio in parts of Alaska, Arizona, California,

Colorado, Montana, New Mexico, Oregon, South Dakota, Washington, Wisconsin, and Wyoming. They broadcast from the Indian nations of Navajo, Pueblo (**pweb**•loh), Apache (uh•**pah**•chee), Lakota (luh•**koh**•tuh), Ute (yoot), Eskimo, Ogallala Sioux (**og**•lah•lah soo), Mohawk, Chippewa (**chip**•uh•wah), and Hoopa (**hoo**•pah).

Since there are more than 500 American Indian tribes in the country, there is a lot more work to do. Tribes are looking at different ways to bring radio to their communities.

American Indian Public Radio Stations Across the Country

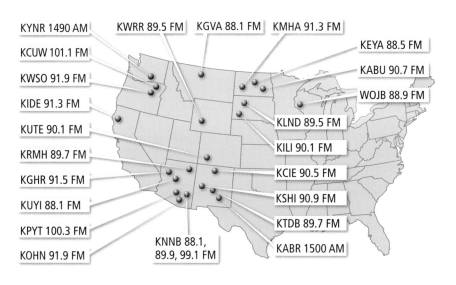

KYNR 1490 AM
KCUW 101.1 FM
KWSO 91.9 FM
KIDE 91.3 FM
KUTE 90.1 FM
KRMH 89.7 FM
KGHR 91.5 FM
KUYI 88.1 FM
KPYT 100.3 FM
KOHN 91.9 FM

KWRR 89.5 FM   KGVA 88.1 FM   KMHA 91.3 FM

KEYA 88.5 FM
KABU 90.7 FM
WOJB 88.9 FM

KLND 89.5 FM
KILI 90.1 FM
KCIE 90.5 FM
KSHI 90.9 FM
KTDB 89.7 FM

KNNB 88.1, 89.9, 99.1 FM
KABR 1500 AM

CHAPTER 4

Native Voices in Native Languages

KABR is another Navajo radio station in New Mexico. It is located about 70 miles from Socorro, New Mexico.

"I am your grandfather," children hear an elderly voice say on KABR. In many American Indian communities, grandparents are not just grandparents to their own grandchildren; they are grandparents to all of the children.

Three Alamo Navajo middle school students hold a KABR sign.

If you do not speak the Navajo language, you may think you will not be able to understand him. But, if you listen closely to the inflection in his voice, you may be able to understand. Grandparents all seem to sound the same and say the same things to their grandchildren. He is saying, "Listen to your teachers and do what your parents ask you to do."

He is giving them advice. He is also teaching them. By speaking to the children in Navajo, he is helping them learn the Navajo language. He is a fluent Navajo speaker.

Indian radio stations across the country broadcast in both their native languages and in English.

In Bethel, Alaska, KYUK presents its daily news programs in English and in the native language Yup'ik (**yoop**•ik).

KILI on the Pine Ridge Reservation in South Dakota broadcasts in the Lakota language every morning.

KTDB, the radio station run by the band of Ramah Navajo in Pinehill, New Mexico, broadcasts more in the Navajo language than it does in English.

Keeping native languages alive is very important. Languages help you look at the world around you from different perspectives. Nancy Martine-Alonzo, an American Indian leader in New Mexico, says that KTDB helps to keep the Navajo language alive. This is very important for young people. Like all languages, Navajo is used for teaching, business, law, and communicating to children about how to behave.

Richard Begay holds up a Navajo-language book.

Nancy Martine-Alonzo (holding the book) and American Indian teachers and educators at the University of New Mexico, College of Education

In the English language, your mother may tell you to make your bed and clean up your room. In the Navajo language, the Navajo mother will tell her children to walk in beauty.

In English, you are given a specific order. In Navajo, you are told to behave a certain way that will make you beautiful along with everything else that is beautiful in the world.

You might ignore your mom's order in English and not clean your room. You might instead pay more attention to the Navajo instruction and *want* to clean your room.

Nancy Martine-Alonzo is a leader in the field of American Indian education for the state of New Mexico. She explains that the Navajo language helps children value beauty. She says that Navajo values and belief systems are part of the Navajo language.

New laws are being crafted on national and state levels around the country to save native languages. People are looking at different ways of doing this. Community radio is a useful tool.

Something to Know

In the Navajo language, people call the Navajo Nation *Diné Bikéyah* (Dih•**nay** Bi•**kay**•yah).

CHAPTER 5

Programming on American Indian Radio Stations

"We are just like you; we are the same," says Burton Poley from his office in Albuquerque, New Mexico. Poley is the manager of the Native Voices One organization, called NV1 for short. NV1 provides satellite programming to American Indian radio stations across the country.

Burton Poley sits at his desk at the headquarters of NV1. Behind him is a large sign announcing Indian news and music.

Just like non-Indian radio stations, Indian radio stations can play hip-hop, rap, rock-and-roll, and country and western music. Just like radio stations in cities, Indian stations inform people to use their seat belts, to register to vote, and to drive carefully. But there are differences. Listening to an American Indian station, you may hear what is happening in Iraq and Washington, D.C. You may also hear that someone has lost a cow, that there's a good deal on hay at a nearby ranch, or that there's a rodeo coming up.

American Indian stations often feature people from the communities. At KSHI, the radio station for the Zuni tribe in New Mexico, station manager Duane Chimini regularly has children from the Zuni school on the air.

Duane Chimini smiles as he sits at his digital editing station at the KSHI radio station in the Zuni Pueblo of New Mexico.

"This morning on KSHI, I have several kindergarten students with me today. They are going to tell you what they are learning in school. And, they are going to tell you what they would like you to do," he tells his listeners.

Five children crowd around the microphone. The children tell their audience that they are learning to read and write. They say that they want everyone to read to them.

To continue his program, Duane may announce an upcoming Parents' Day at Zuni High School, then dedicate a song to the teachers at the Zuni School, and play a special request—"Powwow Girl." This is a hip-hop song about a young girl who dances at powwows. *Powwows* are American Indian social dances held around the country.

Where Programming Comes From

Like all radio stations, programming on American Indian radio stations comes from many places: satellite services, DVDs, CDs, tapes, and live studio performances. For stations to receive satellite programming, they need to have a satellite dish. With a satellite dish, Indian radio stations can receive programming from Burton Poley's NV1 Satellite Services, just as a cable channel receives Disney programming.

Syndicated Radio

When a news program is offered through a satellite to many stations, it is **syndicated.**

Francis Montoya, a member of the San Felipe and Isleta tribes in New Mexico, was one of the first to develop a syndicated Indian radio show. Francis now hosts *Singing Wire* every Sunday on KUNM radio in Albuquerque, New Mexico. *Singing Wire* features American Indian music. It is also well known for its interviews with American Indian performers and leaders.

Other News

At 1:00 P.M. every day on KTDB, station manager Barbara Maria and the radio station staff announce international, national, and local news. They also read updates from the Associated Press. The Associated Press is a national news service that is available to all radio stations. Barbara and her staff report the news in both Navajo and English. They tell the community about events going on in Israel, England, and the United States. Then, they bring attention to local news around Pinehill and the surrounding communities.

Students in the KTDB announcer's booth

During the local news, the KTDB announcers may ask if anyone has noticed a lost sheep or horse. They may ask where to buy the best hay, mention a school announcement, or announce a campus cleanup. KTDB also has a homework hotline. If the people of Ramah didn't have KTDB, they would not know what was going on in their own community. They would not know about some things going on in the world. It is the only way they get information. It is the only way they have their voices heard.

25

Sports

American Indian radio also has play-by-play sports. "Yáá'at'ééh (Yaht•ay), Welcome!" the KTDB high school student announcer says in Navajo and English. Then, he begins a detailed rundown of the school basketball game. Sometimes, he may include an English word because there isn't a word in the Navajo language for what he wants to say. The Navajo language is very descriptive. Five Navajo words might be needed to explain one English word.

Broadcasting in an Indian language is very important. It means that everyone will have information. KTDB is the Voice of the People.

Five American Indian children in the Ramah Navajo school gym hold a basketball. They are regular listeners of KTDB.

Tom Bee with his award from the 43rd Annual Grammy Awards, 2001, Los Angeles, CA

Music

If you listen to American Indian music, you will hear many different American Indian voices. One act you are sure to hear is Tom Bee and his band.

In Chapter 8, you will meet Tom Bee. He is a modern-day hero, because nothing kept Tom Bee from having his voice heard.

On American Indian radio stations, you will also hear music by non-Indians. Unlike programming on city radio stations, where one station plays country and another hip-hop, American Indian radio stations typically play a little bit of everything.

CHAPTER 6

Look Who's Running the Radio Station

"Students, here are your assignments for this week," the radio teacher says. "Record satellite programs, edit the story you recorded yesterday, and don't forget to put it in the sign-off cart before shutting down the station today."

Students in middle and high school at the Alamo Navajo radio station, KABR, take on the roles of on-air host, producer, director, and editor. About half of the programming comes from satellite services, and the other half is locally produced. The students enjoy producing their own programs. When they gather stories outside the studio—in their community—they are called *field producers.*

On days when they are in the field, they line up all of their equipment before going out. Their equipment includes a tape recorder, audio tapes and batteries, papers, and pens. They pack all this into a carrying case.

Part of the assignment is to make a list of questions before arriving at a community member's house. This is very important for producing a radio program. Once at a home or a business, students quickly set up their equipment and begin interviewing the people featured in their stories. If a person speaks Navajo, the student asks for responses in both Navajo and English.

Back at the station, the students have a lot to do before their stories are ready to air. First, they must listen to each interview and find the most interesting sound bites. *Sound bites* are short parts of interviews that help to tell stories. Students create scripts around the sound bites. They add their own words to fill in parts of their stories. The part where they tell the story is called *narration.*

Lynnett at KABR radio station

To put it all together, the students record the narration and sound bites, then add music or other sound effects. Then, they take all of these elements and edit them into stories. It's a long process. But it is worth it. The students are helping to tell the stories of the Alamo Navajo community. And this is how their voices are heard.

If you are interested in visiting the Alamo Navajo people in New Mexico, there are many things to see and many things to learn about. If you explore the countryside, you may find arrowheads, stone dwellings, and **petroglyphs.** You will also see that the land is very rugged and isolated from cities and towns.

The ruggedness and isolation of the land helped the Alamo Navajo people in the past by making the people hard to find. If you are interested in visiting the Alamo people, they are no longer hard to find. But the land they live on remains rough and undeveloped. Phone and cable TV companies do not provide service. There is very limited, if any, cell phone service. That's why the radio station is so important.

Here's a Job for You!

Following are some more things students learned how to do at KABR. If you are interested in radio, here are some jobs you should learn about, too.

The *station manager* makes sure that the station runs properly and that programming is on the air when it should be. There are many other things the station manager must do. The station manager makes sure that there is enough money to run the station, that there are programs to air, and that the station crew knows how to operate the equipment.

The *programmer* schedules the shows that are going to be on the air. The programmer determines whether the right type of program is on the air at the right time of day. The programmer takes cues for scheduling from the people who are listening. News is usually early in the morning and at lunchtime, because people can tune into it as they drive to work or have a lunch break. A show about math may be on at 10 A.M., when students are in class.

The *news director* runs the news department. The news director also assigns stories to reporters who go out and collect the news from community members.

The *producer* is the person who creates the stories. The producer thinks of stories that are important to the audience. Then, the producer interviews different people to get ideas about the stories. Once the interviews are recorded, the producer edits the stories down to a specific amount of time.

With a Little Help from Your Friends

KUNM Radio at the University of New Mexico in Albuquerque offers American Indian and non-Indian students the opportunity to learn how to produce radio programs. At KUNM, students produce a live weekly program. Philip Riley, a high school student from the Acoma Pueblo in New Mexico, is a member of the radio crew. The show is part of a training program called the Youth Radio Project. The weekly show often features youths who are leaders in the community. Mescla Experience, a youth band, appeared on one of its shows. Different cultures influence this band's music.

The *editor* is the person who takes information that is recorded on an audiotape and cuts the information down to make a story.

The *publicist* is the person who tells the public what is going to be on the air. The publicist creates a program schedule and sends out public notices.

Paoli and Philip (below) talking into microphones

Youth musician and activist Jaime Espinosa of Mescla Experience, during an interview on Philip Riley's show on KUNM Radio in Albuquerque, New Mexico

The Youth Radio Project is one way American Indian students are learning how to work in radio. This experience will help them to have a voice heard by others in the United States.

CHAPTER 7

Red Tape and Orange Barrels

You may have heard the term "cutting through red tape." It's an old English saying. It is believed to have come from an English practice of tying government files with red tape. The only people who could move and cut the red tape to get to a file were workers who were not high up in the government. When a file needed to be opened, they would need to find the worker to cut the red tape. This would take a lot of time. So, when things move slowly because of too many rules, people often say, "Let's cut through the red tape." What they mean is, "Let's make this happen," or, "Let's do it ourselves."

Other things can happen to slow things down. In Albuquerque, New Mexico, traffic often slows down because there are orange barrels in the road. The barrels usually mean the government is working on a road. To get from one side of town to another, people have to drive around numerous orange barrels.

American Indian tribes have cut through lots of red tape. And, like the drivers dodging barrels, they have had to work around many things to start radio stations and keep them running.

It takes a lot of money to run a radio station. It also takes a lot of knowledge.

In order to run a radio station, you need money to pay the staff. The staff usually consists of the manager, producers, and technicians. Then, you need money to buy programming. And there are costs for your heating, electricity, and phone.

In the city, private radio stations make money from advertising. Most of the money that helps to run a public radio station comes from businesses and the people who listen to the station.

Businesses that support public radio stations are called *underwriters.* This is probably a new word for you, so let's look at it more closely. As underwriters, businesses give money to the station. Then, the station puts a message on the air about the underwriter's business. You have probably heard these messages. They sound like this: "This program is brought to you in part by your local car dealer."

These messages are different from commercials in that they cannot offer to sell anything. That is why people call public radio stations *noncommercial* stations.

Listeners who give money to their public radio station are called *members.* The members of public radio stations are regular people, just like your mom and dad. Members donate money to the public radio station to help keep it on the air. They do this because being a member is a good thing for their community. They are helping their public radio stations. All public radio stations need help.

You might ask, "Why don't they go to businesses outside their community for money? Why not ask them to be underwriters?"

Those are good questions. Most American Indian radio stations don't broadcast to cities and towns. They are in the country, not the city. If the people who buy things from stores can't hear the radio stations, it is not going to help the stores to advertise on the radio. It would be bad business for them to underwrite a show their customers can't hear.

In cities, people also have many different job opportunities. Many people in the city make a lot of money, and they can afford to give some of it away. They like giving it to public radio.

Public radio gives people a lot of good information. Maybe your parents give money to the public radio station in your community. In large cities, with many people giving money to their public radio station, the station doesn't have to worry so much about paying all its bills.

In American Indian communities, however, there are not as many job opportunities. Many people don't make a lot of money. They can't afford to give their money away.

American Indian communities do not have many businesses. In many American Indian communities, there are only a few stores. Those few stores don't need to have messages on the air. Everyone in the community, at one time or another, shops at the local stores on the reservation. They have to because other stores are too far away.

American Indian radio stations can get money from the federal government. Getting money from the federal government is not easy. It involves lots of red tape and many orange barrels. This is probably why only 31 (out of 500) tribes have public radio stations.

Money is one major challenge to American Indian radio stations. Another major challenge is correcting misperceptions and stereotypes about American Indian history, issues, and events.

American Indian radio helps people learn about American Indian culture and how it is the same and different from non-Indian cultures. Let's look at how KTDB corrected misperceptions and provided accurate information when an outbreak of a mysterious disease began on the Navajo Reservation in 1993. The cause of the disease was a **hantavirus.** Both Navajo and non-Navajo people got sick and died soon afterward. Sadly, one of the first people who died was a young Navajo man who was about to be married. Then, non-Indian tourists visiting Albuquerque got sick and died. It was very scary for everyone.

Barbara Maria and the staff of KTDB were the first to report the full story of the hantavirus. Because of their reports, major television networks like NBC, ABC, and CNN realized they needed to visit the Ramah Navajo radio station. Once the reporters from the major networks in the country learned the facts, they shared them with the country. If it hadn't been for Barbara Maria and her staff, they couldn't have done this.

Because KTDB provided the facts about the hantavirus, people learned what caused the disease. They learned how to prevent other infections. The reports saved many lives.

This is only one example of how American Indian radio has provided the right information. When there are more American Indian radio stations, everyone will be better off. We all need the right information.

Barbara Maria announcing on KTDB

CHAPTER 8

New Ways to Hear American Indian Voices

As we have discussed, there are more than 500 American Indian tribes in the United States. Thirty-one tribes have built public radio stations. So, there are many more radio stations to be built. Many tribes, however, have found it too difficult to work around all the red tape and orange barrels to build radio stations, so they are looking at other ways to have their voices heard.

Let's see what three American Indian leaders think. What are some good ways for tribes to share information? What needs to happen to have American Indian voices heard?

Leonard Tsosie—A Hogan Hero

Leonard Tsosie is a state senator from New Mexico. He is a member of the Navajo Nation. He speaks both Navajo and English fluently. He started a project to help Navajo people gain access to Internet radio. The project is called Internet to the Hogans. A *hogan* is a traditional Navajo home. It does not have electricity or phone service.

There are many people involved in Internet to the Hogans. It is a very important effort, because few American Indian families have access to the Internet, especially families who traditionally live in hogans. Senator Tsosie wants their voices to be heard.

Through Senator Tsosie's project, Navajo people will be able to get Internet radio. People call Senator Tsosie a "hogan hero" because he is helping American Indian people—even those who still live in hogans—have their voices heard.

Nakonah, a middle school student, Senator Leonard Tsosie, and Dan Chavez stand in front of Dan Chavez's hogan. Senator Tsosie is showing them how to access a Web page.

Elsie Secatero from the To'Hajiilee (**toh**•haj•ih•lay) community is a Navajo speaker.

"Our grandmothers and grandfathers need to have programming in the Navajo language. It's not fair that they can't understand the news or information everyone else can," he says. Senator Tsosie would like to see programs such as *Sesame Street* translated into the Navajo language. That way, Navajo children could learn English and Navajo at the same time.

Some American Indian communities are receiving news in both their languages through Internet radio. Two tribal members of the Red Lake Band of Ojibwe (oh•jib•**way**) in Minnesota founded one of the first Internet radio stations. Their radio names are "Rez Dawg" and "Emcee Edge." They started the station in their house. Internet radio stations are a good idea because they are less expensive than building a broadcast station. But, American Indian communities need to have Internet access to receive the broadcasts. As of 2006, only ten percent of American Indian families had access. That is why Internet to the Hogans and other programs like it, are so important.

Gary Farmer—a Radio Hero

Gary Farmer is a member of the Cayuga (kahy•**yoo**•guh) Nation in Canada. You may have seen him on television or in the movies. He starred in the movies *Ghost Dog: The Way of the Samurai, Smoke Signals, Dead Man,* and *Powwow Highway.* He also appeared on the TV series *Tales from the Crypt.*

Actor Gary Farmer at his art gallery in Santa Fe, New Mexico

43

Like Jay Silverheels, Gary Farmer has done a lot to help make Indian voices heard. Farmer helped to start many radio stations in Canada. In Canada, they are called aboriginal radio stations. *Aboriginal* means "native" or "first." Canadian Indians lived in Canada before anyone else.

Farmer has also supported American Indian radio stations. He would like to see radio stations in every Indian community. He points out that if you made a dot for each Indian community on a world map and then connected those dots, they would circle the world. He says that if each of these communities had radio stations, then Indian voices would be heard around the world.

Today, it is possible for this to happen because of **technology.** Technology is making many things happen that weren't possible before. Soon, every television and radio station in the country will have a new way of broadcasting. Radio and television stations will become **digital.** Cell phones and personal music players already are.

Senator Tsosie and Farmer know that there is a lot of red tape to cut through and orange barrels to go around in order for American Indian voices to be heard. It is not an easy task, but new technology will help make it possible.

Tom Bee—A Music Hero

Music has always provided a way for voices to be heard. Tom Bee was one of the first musicians to help make American Indian voices heard.

Tom Bee is an extraordinary person. Without any money or knowing anyone, he went to Los Angeles from New Mexico to get his music recorded. He was a very shy 15-year-old with a speech impediment. He had to get over his stuttering before he could talk to people in the music business. When he realized he didn't stutter when he sang, he began to sing a lot. He turned a disability into an ability.

Tom Bee says that nothing has been easy for him. He says you can achieve anything if you believe in yourself—even when no one believes in you. He also says you have to have dreams, but that you can't be just a dreamer. You have to be a dreamer and a doer! He also says, "Don't take no for an answer."

After lots of work, Tom Bee became very famous. He won major awards for his songs. His band is called XIT. Their songs, "Plight of the Redman," "Silent Warrior," and "Relocation" tell of the American Indian struggle for independence and justice. Tom Bee and his band are more than entertainers. They are voices for American Indian people. 45

Tom Bee at his record company Sounds of America (SOAR) in Albuquerque, New Mexico.

Through radio stations and new technology, American Indian tribes are making their voices heard across the country—all you have to do is tune in. If you do, you will hear the best in hip-hop, rap, rock-and-roll, and traditional American Indian music.

You will hear news that ranges from the local community to the international sector. You will meet some of today's great American Indian leaders—leaders such as Barbara Maria, Nancy Martine-Alonzo, Francis Montoya, Tom Bee, Senator Leonard Tsosie, and Gary Farmer. These American Indian leaders are modern-day foot runners. They are helping to make American Indian voices heard—through radio and beyond.

Glossary

broadcast: to send a signal from a television or radio station

digital: a way of recording information that allows text, sound, or video to be stored as numbers

hantavirus: a group of viruses carried by rodents that cause severe lung infections in people

petroglyphs: pictures that are carved, pecked, chipped, or painted into stone, often depicting stories about past events

sidekick: partner

sovereign nation: an independent nation. American Indian tribes are sovereign nations. American Indians have dual citizenship. They are citizens of their tribes, and they are citizens of the United States.

stereotyping: believing something about a people or a culture that may be true, untrue, or partially true

syndicated: available for broadcast in many areas

technology: a set of tools that help people communicate and do things faster or better

INDEX